ON BECOMING A SURVIVOR

ON BECOMING A SURVIVOR

A PSYCHOLOGIST WHO SURVIVED
VIOLENT CRIME PROVIDES
COMFORT
AND
GUIDELINES FOR SURVIVORS, THEIR
FAMILIES & FRIENDS

Dr. Barry Ward Reister

2003

BRIEF AUTHOR BIOGRAPHICAL INFORMATION:

Dr. Barry Reister did his undergraduate work at the University of Kentucky and received his doctoral training at Indiana University. In between those two institutions, he served as a Lieutenant with the Armored Cavalry and spent one year in Vietnam. He has served as a Staff Psychologist and Assistant Director of University Counseling Services at Boston College and later became Director and Assistant Dean for Counseling and Health Services at Loyola Marymount University in Los Angeles, Dean of Student Affairs at Queens College, C.U.N.Y., Director of one of the model Counseling Centers in the nation at Illinois State University, and finally Associate Dean of the Graduate School at Cameron University. In all of these positions, he also held a faculty position teaching graduate students. In addition, he also held faculty positions at Northeastern University, the University of Southern California, and Columbia University where he also taught graduate students. He also conducted a small scale private practice while in all of the positions mentioned above. He has also published widely in professional Journals. He now has a private practice in his hometown of Lexington, Kentucky.

TABLE OF CONTENTS

I would like to thank the following people for their contributions:
Detectives Broad and Stracky
Jim Brinegar
Hank Durand
Lula Johnson
Renita Knox
Noel Miller
Julia Reister Moore
Mildred Reister
Ward Reister
Anne Rezzo Rosen
Susan Harper Slate
My appreciation also goes to other friends and colleagues who supported me through out this process.

INTRODUCTION

You've just been through a major trauma in your life. Whatever you've felt victimized by, be it a mugging, a theft, a burglary or bodily injury, you have been hurt both physically and psychologically. After all, you learned growing up that your parents or guardians would protect you from danger or teach you how to protect yourself from danger. You were told to watch both ways before crossing the street and to not take candy from strangers. You have been functioning fairly well out there in the world. You've learned which situations to avoid. For instance, "You won't catch me walking down any back alleys at 2 a.m."

You've also probably learned the world is generally a pretty okay place where people treat others with a fair amount of consideration. You believed the world was a "safe place," and now, like a bolt of lightning, out of the sky, you've become a victim of violent crime! I would like, hereafter, to refer to you as a survivor of violent crime. You have survived, you're alive to read this, and you shall overcome your current feelings of trauma and hurt.

Rape victims some time ago began referring to themselves as survivors, and I think the word is most empowering. So from now on you are a survivor of violent crime! <u>YOU ARE A SURVIVOR!</u>

OVERVIEW OF SOCIETAL PERCEPTIONS OF VIOLENT CRIME

If you think about your Wednesday night television thriller, it usually starts with the commission of the crime. The victim (usually a murder victim) may be addressed very quickly by a faded picture in a high school yearbook and never heard from again in the course of the "thrilling" show. The focus is then on the good guys and the bad guys or the people in the white hats and the black hats, with guns and with power.

Often times, people, due to their own needs for feeling safe, want to focus on the event. So, for instance, if you had your house burglarized, your neighbor would be much more likely to inquire how they got in and what they took rather than how you're feeling about having been violated.

I think there are reasons why these Wednesday night thrillers grip their audiences and why your neighbor inquires about what was stolen. This is because of primal fears and concerns about the bolt of lightning that comes out of nowhere, with no warning, and zaps you!

What these thrillers provide their viewers is an opportunity to have a sense of control over the bolt of lightning. Also, the reason people inquire about the burglary is so they can feel safe because they don't have that kind of window, or they always use their deadbolt, or they plan to change those aspects of their house that are identical to yours. So, again, it's your neighbor's way of dealing with their own sense of vulnerability that causes them to focus on the event as opposed to your feelings.

Again, I think it is a primal issue, and it strikes chords deep within the survival mechanisms of each of us.

So, there are understandable reasons why our society has been desensitized to the survivors of violent crime. Knowing this does not make it any easier for survivors, but it might assist us as we educate friends and family about how we're feeling and what we need. I find that people are very willing to "be there" for each of us when, in fact, they know and understand what it is we want and need.

YOUR STORY

"Talk To Me"
Little Willie John

I think it's important to tell your story. You need to tell your story in as much detail as you like and as many times as you like. The process of telling your story gives you a sense of control over events you have felt very little control over.

Realize that your events, in an objective sense, may seem more or less severe than mine. Realize that whether your purse was snatched, your house burglarized, you were physically harmed (perhaps even brutally), or had your life threatened with a gun or knife, your subjective experience is valid. You were violated; your feelings are very real.

I would like to further suggest that it might be helpful to you throughout your healing process to keep your own diary. I fully realize this process may begin in the early stages of your recovery, at mid-point in that process, or at the end point of that process. Maybe you'll begin the diary after the healing process is complete. Perhaps, you'll never feel a need to keep a diary, which is all right. This book in some ways could be called my diary.

MY STORY

Mary and I approached her dimly lit parking lot at precisely midnight of Good Friday. We had been to a movie and were returning from dinner with a "doggy bag" of spaghetti and clam sauce on the front floorboard.

We stopped and were kissing good night. Over her left shoulder, I saw a van pull up beside us with two, well-groomed, young men. The driver had combed back hair and a prominent chin. This was the best profile view of him I would have. I felt nothing threatening in the occurrence of two guys pulling up and parking just like we were, perhaps to visit a friend.

They suddenly rushed us. I flicked the automatic door lock and got a flash of a frontal look at the van driver, over the barrel of a .38 caliber revolver. Holding the pistol with two hands in a semi-crouched firing position, he appeared tense, and I saw him nervously alternating from one foot to the other, like a linebacker in a football game waiting for the snap. My thoughts simultaneously switched gears to Mary's ex-husband who had, during their marriage history, brutally beaten her. I remembered the story Mary had told me of an incident during her college years. Her future husband had waited for her then boyfriend, outside her dormitory with a loaded gun, and had attempted that same night to run over him. I remembered Mary making allusions to her ex-husband's possible family relations with organized crime. I calculated that his verbal threats to kill her if she ever left him were about to become a tragic reality.

The profile of Mary's ex-husband is clearly of a very unstable, insecure man who values violence as a way of dealing with his own frustrations and inadequacies. It flashed through my mind that this time he had really gone off the deep end. He had hired a killer. In this parking lot two senseless cold-blooded murders were going to take place. I knew Mary's ex-husband was unstable, but I didn't realize he was crazy. As it turned out this was an act of unbridled, random violence from two members of an L.A. gang. It certainly had nothing to do with Mary's ex-husband or any other third party.

I threw myself over Mary and screamed, "What the hell is going on?" I reached over and opened the passenger door to make a futile attempt to limit the crime to armed robbery. "Take our car, take our money, and leave us alone." Compressed into the next two hours was all the fear and anger I had experienced as a combat officer in Vietnam. In Vietnam, at least, I was armed and always alerted to danger, but this was my home turf, the place where I expected to be able to live without being attacked.

On Mary's side, the second armed attacker ordered me to open my door where the van driver, apparently the leader of the gang, was waiting with an experienced hand to take my watch, my most valuable keep-sake, given to me by my dad. He said, "Don't look, punk! Get in the back seat and put your head down." While he was taking my wallet and Mary's purse, I figured, "If we're lucky, they're through with us." Clearly, we were not going to be lucky.

Mary and I were now, as directed, lying face down in the back seat and I heard her whisper, "I'm sorry sweetie." Mary and I will both be put through hell before we will have another face to face encounter.

The gun was now being pressed firmly to my temple in several places as though he were looking for the opening to go completely through. "Punk, I'll kill you and you too, bitch."

When our car started, I knew this was going to get a lot worse. We were probably headed for the field behind the airport where the plane noise would drown out any gunshots. I thought, "If they shoot, it should be a fairly painless death. Suddenly, there will just be lights out." I wonder where they'll find our bodies and imagine the shock and sadness of my parents, sister, and two nieces.

While one attacker was taking the van to a different location, the other followed him in our car while still holding the gun to my head. Later, reunited in crime, the van driver jumped into the back seat. He got in and what I heard made painfully clear their next step. I heard a zipper and, "All right do it." Mary said, "No way." At that point I thought the pistol at my temple might actually puncture my head, as he said, "Do it or I'll kill him! Do it right now or I'll kill him"!

I heard sounds. Sounds normally associated with tenderness, intimacy, and love, were now being heard in nightmarish atmosphere of violence and pure hatred. "Lick my balls, bitch," he ordered.

After a few minutes, the driver ordered me to direct him to my bank, and the attacker told Mary to take her pants off. He kept yelling, "Don't look! Don't look, bitch!" Mary's foot by my face told me he had positioned her on top of him facing away, and I heard him say, "Now ride it…what's that?" "I'm having my period." "Then take it out. Now ride it!"

My insides, at this point, felt like a raging volcano ready

to erupt. Mary, whom I'd been dating for a couple of months, is one of the sweetest, most loving women I have ever known. She is the mother of three young children. One of the first things I remembered her pleading when this nightmare began was, "Please don't kill me. I have three little kids." This gentle soul, after six years of a personally violating marriage, is being raped in my presence, and I'm held powerless to protect her. If I go for the gun that vacillates from my head to my neck to the heart region of my chest, if I'm successful in getting the gun, what about the other gun? So, they'll use Mary as a hostage and we'll have a gunfight in the back seat. There clearly is no option for action on my part without great risk to my life or Mary's…and most probably both.

We're at a traffic light now, and what sounds like teenagers in the car next to us start yelling, "Go for it." They are obviously seeing glimpses of the rape and misinterpret what is going on as a couple that couldn't wait until they got home.

After going too far on Lincoln Boulevard and missing my bank, they turned off on a dark side street. Now, it was time to have Mary change position and perform fellatio on the attacker in order to bring him to orgasm. At this point, I can only think of him as a poor pathetic animal turned mean. I would like to pull his brains out through his eye sockets, but I've been rendered powerless. Moved to the front seat with my head down, the attackers switched places to start this same tortuous routine again. My most painful recollection was the rocking of the car as the second attacker raped Mary. I heard her stifled moans of pain and the first attacker's raucous laughter as he responded to the back seat action and simultaneously pushed the pistol intensely to my head.

If one could die of an adrenaline overdose, I would have been dead at this point. What kept running through my head was that our only chance of survival was to act calm.

I was aware as we proceeded that my car had been very low on fuel when the evening started. I had just bought a new car, and my Oldsmobile had been for sale. Mary had never ridden in the Olds, and I thought it would be fun to take her out in this car that felt like you were riding in your living room. I mentioned to the driver that he really should get some gasoline. I could think of nothing worse than these two tense animals with guns to our heads, out of gasoline and feeling desperate. He said, "Shut-up, punk, or I kill you!"

He was now getting agitated because he couldn't seem to find his way. I told him that if I could sit up, I could locate where he was and give him better directions. He finally conceded with the recurrent warning, " Don't look at me punk, I kill you. If you taking us to the cops, man, I kill you."

We got out at the Ready-Teller, and he, of course, kept the gun in his pocket just like on your TV thriller. I withdrew two hundred dollars, but he persisted, "I want more punk, or I kill you." I then said something I had said a couple of times earlier. In my calmest psychologist's voice I said, "All I want to do is to help you get what you need tonight." I had thought the upper limit was $200, but I tried again, and $200 more appeared. "More man, I kill you. I swear." Another $200 appeared, but not a fourth. The bank had just raised the Ready-Teller limit on weekends to $600. The film on the Ready-Teller camera had run out, we later discovered.

This was the second time I had given any thought to escaping, but that would have felt like abandoning Mary. The first time was when I was by the front door. I was also right by the door handle. Now, we're at a bank that is a part of a shopping center where 100 yards away is a well-lit grocery store. I could just run for it, but leave Mary alone? NO WAY was this an option. "You've got the money. Take the car and leave us here." "Shut up punk, I kill you!" In retrospect I realized this guy sure was consistent in his dialogue with me, a bit on the simplistic side, but certainly consistent. Mary and I have engaged in a lot of this type of black humor around our trauma which has been sanity saving at times.

Now, we are moving into the home stretch of my story. The events since the beginning have taken about an hour and a half. Are they now looking for a place to shoot us? Who knows, but we were again driving. Mary had her head down in the back seat, and I was in the front seat with my head down. The man in the back seat is now talking about their gang nicknames. He is KILLER and his friend is PSYCHO. He said that wouldn't help us with the police. In an attempt to placate them, I said, "We won't tell the police anything." At this point the driver struck me in the back of the head with the barrel of the pistol. "Shut up punk.. I don't like white people." From the rear I heard, "Yea, we're gonna shoot your dick off."

Throughout this ordeal, every time I got pushed with the gun or threatened, I remember using a consciously induced relaxation response despite the racing adrenaline. I recall taking deep breaths, exhaling completely, and voluntarily relaxing the muscles of my arms and shoulders.

As I feel the warm blood come out of my head, down

my neck, and around the back of my ears, I reach for my handkerchief. "What are you doing punk? Trying to catch the blood? Don't be worried about a little blood. You're gonna be dead in a few minutes. Do you have kids?" "No." "Oh, you're really dead meat now!"

At two other points in the evening I had asked about my watch, explaining it was worthless except for the sentimental value to me. Each inquiry had been met with, "Shut up punk. I kill you!" I thought I would give it one more try which was met with, "If you mention that watch one more time, I'm gonna splatter your brains all over that door!" Brains-watch-brains-watch—I decided to let the watch go.

Suddenly, they pulled to the side of the road and told Mary to get out, adding, "You'll never see him alive again."

Earlier, with Mary in the car, I knew a possibility of their threatening was to get her to comply with their requests. Now, Mary was safe and they continued ranting, "You're dead meat now." "We're gonna kill you punk." Suddenly, they pulled over and said, "Get out!"

Asphalt never felt so good! I watched as the two misguided, hate-filled men drove away with the driver as the chauffeur and the other person in the back seat as the chauffeured. I had a quick glimpse of how sad and disempowered their lives must be to be driven to get a glimpse of power in this violent way, violating the lives of innocent survivors for two hours of domination.

I, however, did not tarry long on this reflection. I was quickly on my feet. Feeling the blood run out of the back of my head while I was running across the freeway, I put one hand on a barbed wire, six feet fence and jumped it. This was not something in everyday life that I do, or would ever think I could do. "Mary, Mary, is she OK?" I'm thinking as I'm running. We have been let out on the same stretch of road. I'm scanning the other side of the road, as I'm running, bleeding, and feeling tears of joy running down my cheeks that we're both still alive. I'm also trying to flag down passing cars at 2 AM but no one stops. Suddenly, I find myself thinking, "Surely, to God, they won't circle back to do me in." I started watching the approaching cars, hoping I wouldn't see my own.

After a couple of miles, I saw Mary looking like a scared, stunned dog that had been hit by a car. Two men were standing outside of their car, and two women from a different car were standing at an even further distance at a roadside call phone.

Only by the imprints in my hand and some pain in my left foot, could I know that I could once again vault over this fence. I was so happy to see Mary that I think I could have walked through the fence to get to her.

"Mary, Mary we're alive! We're alive! Mary, we're alive! We're alive!" I hugged her and kissed her, but she pulled away from the kiss, being sensitive to what had in fact been in her mouth that night...along with her own vomit in response to their actions.

I called the state police from the roadside call phone and reported the stolen car, license number and location last seen. We then went to the hospital with the two men who had stopped. They had, in fact, passed Mary once and circled back realizing something serious had happened. Mary and I were touched by these two men's obvious compassion and willingness to help.

After two hours at the hospital, where Mary and I were examined and treated, we had to wait two more hours for the police to come and take a report. I knew the reason the police took so long was that we were alive, and there were many more life-threatening things going on out there in the world for police to attend to.

It was now 6 a.m. and we were heading home. It seemed to make the most sense to me to try and retrace the route of the van, which had approached us six hours earlier, while that memory was fresh. We helped the police find the van. The fingerprints from it were critical evidence at the pretrial hearing. On arriving at Mary's house, we met this small group of three little confused faces that are Mary's children. Fortunately, her babysitter was a neighbor and was able to spend the night. After rejoicing at being alive, feeling angry at having to rejoice at being alive, and shedding a few more tears, I left Mary with some loving, supportive neighbors and family members. I went to the home of Hank, my boss and friend, and had a stiff glass of scotch…not my usual breakfast. I told Hank and his wife of the series of events I had been through. I remember telling them that I want to go out someplace and make a contribution in response to the meaningless actions of these two hopeless people. I never believed it feasible that either of these guys would ever be caught. I remember how weird it felt to suddenly realize I had no wallet, no identification, and no money. Hank's wife loaned me twenty dollars, and they drove me home. I told my story to my neighbors and called my parents, my sister, and a good friend from high school and related the events of the day to them. After having told my story at least six times, I went to sleep on my neighbors' couch. They knew that with a head wound it's best to wake the person at regular intervals. They did this to assure that more serious head trauma had not occurred. In the event of serious injury and psychological trauma, it's probably best for all of us not to be alone.

The next day Hank said, "You know, if anybody ever asks me how I could ever leave this town, I'm going to tell them what happened to you. The fact is that it's so common place, it didn't even make the paper."

Whatever you do, find close family and friends and tell your story as many times as you need to.

TRAUMATIZED STAGE

" Shattered, My Life's Been Splattered"
Mick Jagger

You may well be in what I like to call the smashed or pulverized stage of recovery right now. To me, it felt like being the character, Tom, in a Tom & Jerry cartoon. Tom inevitably seems to get flattened or smashed by some devious plan of Jerry's. Then you see this flattened two dimensional character wobbling around, unable to speak, function, or even walk.

You, may well feel in the "Smashed Stage." Here are just a few of the telltale signs.

Mistrust: You used to view the world as a "safe place". Clearly, it is not. In fact, you might even view it as a downright hostile place. Where is it safe to go? What time of the day is safe to be out? Should I carry a weapon? Would mace be sufficient? How about a sound alarm?

You probably feel like you would like to be surrounded by armed militia. Perhaps, the only safe way to travel is in an M-60 army tank, and the only safe way to walk is with an M-16 rifle, carrying at least 3 hand grenades, and wearing a flack vest. It feels like a combat zone out there!!! Be you woman or man, young or old, all of what has been described above is certainly within the realm of possible feelings. You bet trust is an issue for you, because it was one of the main things that was smashed!

Fear and Vulnerability: You may very well be feeling afraid and vulnerable. I remember having an electrician come to my house to install outside lights. I was so afraid and feeling so vulnerable that I greeted him by peering around the corner with my .22 caliber rifle, hardly a warm greeting!

I was afraid that my assailants or their gang members would come to my house to kill me. Despite police assurances that this was not how gangs operated and if they had wanted to kill me they would have, I was afraid. Despite the fact that I was a combat veteran of Vietnam and had experienced my fair share of life-threatening situations, I was afraid. Despite anything you've experienced in the past, remember your sense of trust has been temporarily shattered. It's okay to allow yourself to be afraid for a while, maybe even a long while.

I recall spending hours on the floor between my dishwasher and refrigerator. Most of that time was spent talking on the phone to family and friends. If they had decided to send out a rooftop assassin, they couldn't see where I was in the house with the blinds drawn. Even if they shot randomly, I had metal on two sides and two walls on the other two sides. I spent a good deal of my time on the floor talking on the phone to Jim, a good friend whom I had known since childhood. He was someone I trusted and someone who I sensed could empathize and just hear me.

I knew it was common for survivors to see their assailants all around them: in the grocery store, the post office, anywhere and everywhere. I clearly remember an evening when in the grocery, I noticed a Hispanic young man behind me in the line. What a shame that I immediately felt fear and anxiety. Knowing all of this, I still saw what I was certain were my assailants. I pulled up beside them at a stoplight for a better look to try to make sure they were the ones. The driver turned and, through a closed window, pointed to himself and mouthed, "Who me?" Well, that did it in terms of the positive identification. When the light turned green, I didn't move and they didn't move despite the traffic in front having moved. The anxious cars in back of us began blowing their horns. My assailants moved on, and I got behind them to get their license plate number. When I got in the left lane and turned to my office, I was repeating over and over their license number so I could call and report it. After I reported the sighting, I began thinking the following: I saw them. They saw me see them, and they saw me turn left toward my office. During the abduction, they had asked where I worked; and, with a gun to my head, I told them. Now they have a very clear motive to kill me. They will wait outside the gate to where I work, and when I come out...BANG!

The L.A.P.D. later tracked the car down and discovered that I was seeing assailants all around me. Those were not the same two men.

I called L.A.P.D. back and asked for my detective. I told him, " I need to leave town. I want you to come pick me up, take me home, and stand guard while I pack. Then I need you to take me to the airport." Many police are not yet enlightened enough to be that supportive. Fortunately, for me, he was. He said, "You do whatever you have to do to feel safe, and I'll be right there." I was going out of town in another week to give a talk. So, I called my co-presenter and just left a message for her to pick me up at the airport in San Jose. I called another good friend and left word that I was coming to town and would need a safe place to stay. I was afraid, and I needed to get the hell out of town!

When I arrived at the airport, it was like I had entered

a new land of freedom and had received a breath of fresh air...until I saw my assassin. The gang had, in fact, dispatched a hit-man to follow me to San Jose where I would be shot, and; of course, the connections to them would be lessened. I immediately consulted my more rational mind and said, "He's probably not even getting on the same plane." Not only did he get on the same plane, he sat right behind me.

My assassin had been in conversation with the passenger next to him and had a pleasant expression on his face. Then I looked at him, which evoked one of the coldest, meanest stares in return that I had ever encountered. I also noted a significant scar down the left side of his face. Don't most assassins have cold stares and scars?

Again, consulting my more rational self, I knew that he was most probably not an assassin, but the coincidental circumstances sure were eerie. I was most relieved when after being picked up at the airport by my colleague, I didn't see any cars following us as we drove away. Although, I will have to say, I did look back periodically to check.

<u>Disorientation</u>: I remember taking two hours in the morning to take a shower, shave and get dressed. This is a set of tasks that normally takes me half an hour. I couldn't decide what to wear. Do I take a shower first or shave? It's a wonder I didn't put on my clothes and get in the shower. I needed my mother from Kentucky to come and take care of me. If I had it to do over, I would call her and ask for that support.

Mary recalls the way her landlords found out about the incident. They called her to report that her children were some place they shouldn't be. She is normally very watchful of her children's whereabouts. However, she was oblivious on this day after the incident. She found herself going to the kitchen to put the coffee on, right after she had gone to the kitchen and put the coffee on. Mary remembers, approximately two weeks following our incident, having to reach inside the shower to see if the soap was wet to determine if she had taken a shower or not.

These are things all of us do from time to time, but during the days and weeks following being traumatized, they're likely to occur more frequently.

Feelings of Responsibility: What if when the two bad guys had approached my car, I had just started the engine and put my car in reverse. If I, if I, if I had only!

It is very common and predictable that survivors will second-guess themselves concerning where they were, when they were there, locking doors, starting cars, etc. It may be an inevitable, and perhaps healthy, process that we go through to engage in limited amounts of this behavior. It's like replaying a ball game or debriefing a meeting. The most healing words of advice I was given by my detective were, "Don't second guess anything you did because you are alive to talk about it. You are here, and you are alive!"

If I had started my car, Mary and I might be dead. Decisions in those instances are your best instincts to stay alive. Most importantly, you are alive to talk about it. So, in time, let go of your "what ifs."

Self-Image: It is quite likely that you will have some issues about your self-concept. It's normal to feel differently about yourself. Your trust level in the world has been shattered as well as your sense of self-sufficiency. Are you the same self-reliant person you were?

Of course, the answer is YES, but you may very well go through a period of not feeling quite as self-sufficient. The feelings of fear and vulnerability may also be reminiscent of an earlier period in your life. In some ways this may feel like a regressive experience, back to childhood.

While being whisked away to the airport by the police, I wasn't sure if the "bad guys" might try to come on campus that day and "do me in." I notified Campus Security to be on the "look out" for the car I had seen. While in my office waiting for the police to rescue me, I ordered a sandwich. When the sandwich arrived, the person who delivered it looked puzzled as I opened the door just wide enough to allow the sandwich in. As I peered through this crack in the door, I noticed a couple of my staff members walk by with amused looks on their faces. After closing the door, I realized that I must have appeared a frightened child—not an image I was used to projecting to my staff in my role as Director of Psychological and Medical Services at Loyola Marymount University. I felt embarrassed to have presented myself in this manner. I felt crummy inside, like I was some kind of strange, frightened, caged animal.

In summary, you could say I wasn't feeling really terrific about myself. You may go through stages or periods where you too may feel less than okay about yourself. It's all right to have these feelings. Just be assured they will not last forever. Remember, as a survivor, your self-concept will survive as well.

RECONSTRUCTION STAGE

" On The Road Again"
Willie Nelson

As you may recall from your fifth grade history book, there was a period of reconstruction after the Civil War. We survivors also go through a period of reconstruction in putting our lives back together.

<u>Taking Action and Regaining Your Sense of Power and Control</u>: It felt very empowering to me during the first part of my recovery process to take some action. For instance, I had increased lighting installed outside my house. I had bushes and shrubs trimmed back to minimize lurking places in my yard. These actions gave me a feeling of regained control over my safety and welfare. I also had an alarm system installed in my car—not to protect my car, but because the system also has a panic switch. If anyone approached, I could push the button and have the car go crazy with noise.

Your first steps in taking action may be small ones. Mary gained great delight and a sense of control and power by turning off the teakettle that was whistling. The noise that had previously driven her to distraction was now a sound she was pleased to hear. This was because she could take some action and have control over her environment.

This is important whether you have lights installed so your house looks like a Christmas tree, turn off your whistling teakettle, or take a self-defense course. I gained a great sense of empowerment by taking some action and recommend you explore some ways to take action. However small your initial actions may seem, they may be helpful in your recovery!

Dreams and Fantasies: During the reconstruction stage, dreams and fantasies are certainly areas of your life to notice. Mary and I both had fantasies of doing a variety of evil deeds to our assailants. It was only after a week or so that we shared with each other that we were having these fantasies. Both of us, coming from our Judeo-Christian culture, were feeling guilty for having these fantasies. Let the fantasies flow!

It's important, as your psyche unwinds and debriefs the whole experience, to realize that you're going to have a rage manifest in your fantasies. It's a very healthy way to allow your anger and rage to manifest. The same can be said for dreams. I remember having this very vivid dream of being in a parking lot with the same two assailants chasing me. I had a pistol and was saying to them, "Please don't make me shoot you, but if you come any closer I will." Their demise was realized in my dream. Again, an example of rage manifesting in dreams is a very normal, healthy process that you can expect.

You may also find in your dreams and/or fantasies that you are experiencing just the opposite. You may be reliving the sense of powerlessness by having dreams or fantasies of once again feeling powerless. Again, I think just the emerging of whatever thoughts and feelings do occur is very okay. It's important to give yourself permission to experience these thoughts and feelings. It is also helpful along the way to have support—be that a friend, family member, or therapist to help you talk out your thoughts and feelings.

Some people have problems sleeping after going through a traumatic event. Sleep deprivation can cause alterations in perceptions of reality and normal coping skills. Temporary disruptions in sleep patterns might be expected. If disruptions continue, one should consult a health care professional.

<u>Humor</u>: Mary and I both engaged in a lot of humor even in the days immediately following the incident. One night shortly after the incident, I called Mary and her line was busy. Then I called and there was no answer. Knowing she was going to be there and it was midnight, I feared for her safety. I grabbed my trustee .22 caliber squirrel rifle from Kentucky. I couldn't find the clip with the bullets, but I did locate a handful of bullets. Off I went driving "hell bent for leather." When I reached Mary's house, I grabbed my rifle and ran as though I were back in the rice paddies of Vietnam with my M-16.

I had only one bullet in the chamber. I knocked very loudly on her apartment door and then went up the half flight of stairs by her personal door. I then aimed my rifle at what I was sure would be her captor answering the door.

When I saw Mary's sweet face with sleepy eyes peering out the door, needless to say, I felt relieved. The phone had simply been unplugged. Upon leaving, I bolted "the bullet" out of the chamber and it plopped to the floor. Before I left, I assured Mary, "The first thing you should do if anything strange happens is call the police and then call me." She replied with a smile in her eyes, "Will you drop a bullet on them?" Unlike Barney Fife (the T.V. show deputy of Mayberry who only carried one bullet in his pocket), I did have more bullets in my pocket, but we did take a moment to observe the parallels and have a good laugh.

Another time I called Mary and shared that I would be late because I was being "held up" at the office. At first she had feelings of panic and then, of course, realized the benign use of the phrase.

When we recovered my car, it still had the spaghetti with clam sauce on the front floorboard, as we had left it. We joked about the dishes we might be able to make with the recovered clam sauce.

I called Mary one night when we were going out and I was running about fifteen minutes late. I said, " I'll be over to pick you up in fifteen minutes." She replied, "Great! I'll look forward to seeing you. By the way, who is this?"

Humor, black humor or otherwise, may seem totally inappropriate. If that's the case, don't try to make it happen. What happened to you is clearly not funny. However, if humor helps you cope, don't hesitate to use it.

<u>Be Kind to Yourself</u>: I think it's important during your entire recovery process to take special care of yourself. Be kind to yourself. To a lot of people this may not sound like a big deal. To me, who is generally oblivious to style and fashion, it was a big deal, and it felt like I was giving myself a gift. I often have workaholic tendencies, and during this time, I allowed myself to watch old movies, do light reading, and exercise a lot.

Often after a traumatic event, self-esteem is diminished due to the fact that the survivors incorrectly believe that they are somehow at fault. It is particularly difficult during these times of lowered self-esteem to remember to take care of yourself. You deserve the best! Whenever you consider being kind to yourself...do it!

CALLING IN THE TROOPS

"We All Need Somebody to Lean On"
Bill Withers

Remember Barbara Streisand's line, "People who need people, are the luckiest people in the world." Believe me, regardless of what kind of independent, stiff upper lip type of person you are...YOU NEED PEOPLE! There are all kinds of people you may draw on for a number of reasons.

Family: If you are fortunate enough to have living family in whom you would feel comfortable confiding, they may well be some of the first ones you call. I did, and I was glad.

Friends: It's now time to call on a soul mate, close friend, next-door neighbor, or several people you can lean on. Don't hesitate to call on this person when you need someone to just talk to.

Support Groups: Different ones of us maintain different levels of friendship in our lives. This changes from time to time according to our needs. Also, the level of trust and openness to be vulnerable varies in relationships with family and friends. A support group may be a good resource for you. In the appendix are listed some national resources that may assist you in locating local support groups specifically for survivors of violent crime.

Professional Support: As a licensed practicing psychologist, I have a bias in favor of seeking professional counseling assistance. Many of us in the mental health professions seek counseling at somewhat regular intervals to insure that we stay fine-tuned. Since our work is so personal, we must insure that our personal issues stay separate from our consumers.

Most people make lots of excuses not to seek counseling, e.g., I'm beginning to feel better on my own. I've got lots of good friends to support me. I'm not that bad off. That's just for people who have serious psychological problems, ad infinitum.

Spending time with a trained professional can cut months off your recovery process. I view going into counseling as a gift I give myself. So don't let any of those excuses stand in your way of giving yourself the gift of at least six counseling sessions…and as many after that as you like.

In terms of financially affording it, never let that stop you! Under most health insurance policies, there are provisions for mental health coverage. Most HMO's and PPO's provide counseling services. There are also community mental health clinics all over that provide services on a sliding scale, according to your ability to pay. These scales often go all the way down to zero. In California, there is a victim's fund that provides money for health care including counseling. You may want to inquire in your state through the offices of your Attorney General.

My bias is that an important criterion in selecting a therapist is your personal comfort level. While you certainly want to see a trained mental health professional with at least a master's degree, don't unduly obsess about what credentials the person has in terms of degrees, licenses and titles. I have found that whether a person has an M.D., Ph.D., Ed.D. Psy.D., M.S.W., M.A., or M.S., has little to do with whether she/he is a good counselor or not. So, shop for the trained mental health professional that feels good to you. Find one who respects your dignity and allows, encourages, and facilitates the expression of your feelings about what happened to you.

Other Resource People: You may want to confide and receive support from a person involved in religious life. Any religious leader including a shaman, imam, minister, rabbi, priest, or nun may be a good choice for you as you call on your network of human support. You can use your barber, hairdresser, or anyone from whom you feel support.

A glitch you might encounter with some friends or neighbors is what I describe as the "Oho don't get it on me" syndrome. Sometimes the "stuff" you are sharing is very threatening to other people. Remember, this represents the horrible lightning bolt out of the blue that is a fear of many, and now they know someone who has been struck. This is not the impersonal statistic in the paper or a scene from the eleven o'clock news. This is real life and they know that real live person.

Most people will work through the "Oho don't get it on me" syndrome very quickly and it may never be an issue between you. You can rest assured; however, that your friends and family members will be dealing with some of their own feelings of mortality and vulnerability through your experience as well as concerns about your safety and welfare.

People's willingness to assist and be there for you will be surprising. Reach out and let people support you.

YOUR DAY IN COURT

Often our assailants are never apprehended. The information Mary and I received was that our primary assailant had been apprehended. However, the police had killed the other guy in a different incident. In the event that your assailant is captured you then may encounter many new and varied feelings by going to court and facing your assailant. Your reactions may be mixed. You may feel delighted your culprit has been apprehended but also apprehensive and fearful to confront him or her.

Two days before my court appearance, I got a call from a friend who asked, "Would you like for me to go with you to the hearing?" With my best Barney Fife machismo, I replied, "Naw—that's OK. The detectives and I will take care of the court stuff!"

Of course, at that time, I was not allowing the frightened little boy side of me to be heard clearly. When I finally allowed my frightened self to be heard, I realized I would be facing the person who had committed this heinous crime. There was also the possibility of having gang members in the courtroom. Would they follow me home and do me in? As those fears were allowed to emerge, I called my friend back and said, "You bet! I would love to have you be there in court with Mary and me."

My friend, whose name is Noel, had dealt with a great number of rape survivors. She knew the importance of having support in a courtroom. Once I gave myself permission to ask one friend, I also decided to ask another. So a colleague of mine, Susan, accompanied me as well. As a matter of fact, to address some of my paranoid feelings about being followed, Mary and I drove separate cars to the campus of Loyola Marymount University. There we were picked up by our friend, Susan, in a separate car and driven to the courthouse. After the pre-trial hearing, she drove us back for lunch. We then went to the campus where the three of us walked around for an hour to let time elapse before we left at different times in different cars. I'm sure this was a result of watching both detective movies and spy thrillers, but it made me feel more comfortable. Again, I think it's important for people to do what makes them feel comfortable. It also allowed me, through taking some action, to have a sense of control.

I cannot emphasize enough, the importance of taking a support group to the courtroom. That could be one close friend or family member or however many you feel you need.

Mary and I testified individually. They did not want us to contaminate each other's testimony so they would not allow us to be in the courtroom at the same time. There were six other people who had been traumatized by this "duo," and we each had our turn to testify. I cannot emphasize how good it felt to be in the courtroom and to look out and see my friend, Susan, in the audience. On the outside of the courtroom, my friend, Noel, waited with the one of us that was not testifying. That, also, was of great comfort. The detectives, who I described earlier, also did what I understand is very atypical. Being very sensitive to the pre-trial hearing process, they advised us to just respond clearly with short answers and to tell the truth. One was in the courtroom while the other stayed in the lobby with those of us who were waiting.

The person I was going in to testify against was the primary "bad" guy in our incident. I remember standing outside the courtroom with Mary and Noel. I was telling them how nervous I was. I remember being called to testify. Then something changed. I walked into that courtroom like a man on fire. I remember approaching the bench, taking my testimony, and taking my seat. I looked at the man I was testifying against. He gave me a few furtive glances but primarily looked at the floor. Things were very different than what my anxiety, laden body allowed me to think while waiting outside the courtroom. Your anxiety level may be very different than mine, but my hope is that you will testify one way or the other. Because how else will justice be done?

My friend, Susan, reported that she was bowled over by the strength of my testimony. Her husband is an attorney, and she relayed to me how much he would appreciate having such a strong witness. Mary also presented herself very strongly and did a veritable job as a star witness. Susan gave us both good marks after observing our testimonies, and I was so grateful to have her there. My point is that even though you feel you could never take the stand, you may be surprised at the strength that will come when needed.

Concerning my fear of having gang members in the audience, there was one person that looked like he could have been a gang member. Since in our society we have relatively open courtrooms, he just wandered in. The bailiff, upon seeing the person, went over and asked him if he had any business there with the trial. He said, "No, just waiting on my own pre-trial hearing." At that point, the bailiff escorted him out. It felt reassuring to see this individual being escorted out.

I mentioned the fact that there were six other victims in addition to Mary and myself. An ironic twist is that one of these survivors was an armed undercover police officer whose beat was to cover gangs. Similar to other survivors, he was coming out of a restaurant when unexpectedly a gun was placed to his head. During his whole ordeal, the gang members did not know that he had a gun. One of the lessons out of this for me was, despite my temptation to buy a gun as a means of self-defense, that a highly trained person can be carrying one and it can be of no value. If someone holds a weapon on you, carrying firearms can be more of a danger than a protection.

At the end of this pretrial hearing the primary offender in our incident received thirteen years as his sentence. I called one of the primary players in the court system, and they assured me he would definitely be serving the entire time in a penitentiary setting with no option for parole.

STAYING SAFE

Invariably, after an incident has occurred, you will quite likely take some extreme measures out of a sense of wanting to feel safe. After my incident, I made certain I arrived home before dark. I often ran from my car into my house where I locked my door immediately. You may remember some of the other reactions I had e.g. sitting on the floor between my refrigerator and dishwasher etc.

Again, I believe this style of overreacting is understandable and that you should give yourself license to take whatever steps you need in order to feel safe. If that style becomes problematic after a time, again, I would recommend talking to a friend or family member you feel close to or seek professional counseling.

Now, after your extreme reaction process has come to an end, you want to take reasonable steps to stay safe. In fact, what we are going to be reviewing are steps that every human being would be better to observe. You don't have to be a survivor to take steps toward safety. Of course, the items I'm going to list are common sense suggestions of which we are all aware. The value in discussing these items is to assist us all in focusing and reminding ourselves.

One principle of staying safe is the time of day that you are out. Daytime is safer than nighttime, but late night is less safe than early evening. A principle I try to live by is to be home by midnight and absolutely no later than 1 A.M.

I make it an automatic habit when I enter my car to lock the doors, day or night. Some suggestions are obvious. For instance, do not pick up hitchhikers, and don't walk down a dark alley at night.

I like to be aware of people around me, particularly at

night. I notice the direction they are walking, their facial expressions, dress, etc. Of course, this will be impacted by where you live. If you live in Lawton, Okla., or Lexington, Ky., this will be manageable. If you live in Manhattan and you're in mid-town at noon, it would be much more challenging.

If you use public transportation, particularly at night, I would rather be on a subway car that had a number of people on it than a car with one or two people. If all subway cars were sparsely populated, I would choose the car where the driver was located.

I recommend moderation in alcohol consumption in general but particularly when you are out. Excessive alcohol use can and will blur your judgment regarding ideas for safety.

Using common sense is a good rule of thumb. For instance, when walking or jogging go with someone. There is safety in numbers. Stay away from isolated areas, and try to stay near streetlights. Avoid shortcuts. Alleys, parks, and parking lots may be dark and isolated. Protect your valuables. Hold your purse or briefcase tightly to your body. In general, it's a good idea not to carry a large amount of cash, and do not flaunt expensive jewelry.

If you are being followed, cross the street, change direction, and keep looking back so the person knows you can't be surprised. Go to a well-lighted area and enter a store, house, or library. Any place where there are lots of people will do. Notice and remember as much as possible about the person so you can give a good description to the police.

If you are held up do not resist. Nothing is worth risking your life. Often, it is difficult to determine if a robber is armed. Should you ever be robbed, it is important to contact the police and give them as complete a description as you are able.

Another bit of advice regarding safety is to keep your doors locked when you are alone...day or night. This is true for both men and women, but it is especially true for women. Do not let strangers into your house! If you have someone coming to visit before you get home, mail a key to that person or hide it in an unusual place. Under your doormat is not a good place. Try, when possible, to avoid isolated bus or train stops. Stay away from the curb until your bus arrives. If possible, sit near the operator of the vehicle and notify him or her of any problems. While in a car, keep the doors locked. Certainly do not pick up hitchhikers, and when possible park in well lighted areas. Always check the back seat before entering your car. Needless to say, but I'll say it anyway, when you park your car, always lock it and take the keys with you.

I'm certain that you can come up with additional tips for safety. Take some time and make a list of tips that apply to you.

BACK TO THE "REAL WORLD" WITH A NEW PERSPECTIVE

"It's My Turn…To Be What I Can Be"

One of the important things to remember about your survival and recovery process is that it is very likely that, on occasion, you will have lapses to earlier stages of surviving. That may come in the form of fantasy, fears, or rage. It may also manifest around trust issues. It's important to realize that this will occur, and it's a very natural and normal part of the recovery process.

No doubt, there may be some adaptive lessons to be learned out of your experience. Out of my experience, for instance, what I learned was not to take people in the night for granted. I'm certainly not advocating being paranoid of strangers, but when I enter a parking lot at night I'm very aware of who's around me. I notice how they're behaving and in what direction they're moving. I do not tarry now when I go to my car in a strange neighborhood. Even in my own neighborhood I watch the people around me. I move directly to my car, get in, lock the door, put the safety belt on, start my engine, and "move out."

I think each of us has to sort out our experience. We must decide what is worth learning and holding on to and what to release and let go of. I certainly don't think it behooves any of us to come out of a traumatic situation and assume that we live in a world that is ready to traumatize us again. There is overwhelming evidence to the contrary—despite the increase of violent crime. For the most part, society in the United States is very peaceful and law-abiding. We just had the unfortunate opportunity to encounter the atypical person in society who generally is dealing with their own feelings of powerlessness by striking out in anger and rage at innocent victims like you and me.

There may also be a desire, as I obviously feel, to find some kind of meaning in the event. That meaning might be doing something like I'm trying to do, by sharing thoughts and feelings that might be of assistance to others. It might mean writing a letter every time you hear of someone in your community who has been subjected to a similar incident. You could also provide volunteer peer counseling to your police department under the supervision of a mental health professional. Your mode of expression may also manifest in ways that are more tangential than directly related. For example, having developed an increased compassion for people who have been injured or are less fortunate in any way, you might work with the elderly, physically and emotionally challenged, or youth in your community. The time, energy, and attention you give could be of invaluable assistance and have meaningful impact in their lives. In whatever way you may choose to express yourself, in your desire to find meaning in the event, the important thing is that it is meaningful to you.

It's certainly very okay if you have no need to do anything whatsoever to have this event have meaning in your life. In many ways it seems meaningless, and you may be able to leave it there. That can also be a healthy response to the event depending on your own individual preference.

You have survived a horrible ordeal. Sometimes, survivors carry an existential sense of guilt for having survived. If you feel plagued in any way by guilt, seek counseling to work it through. Sometimes, survivors have problems in interpersonal relations that are different than those previously encountered. If these problems exist and persist, again, I would recommend counseling to assist you in resolving these problems.

As I began this book I started out by saying that I would like to refer to you as a survivor of violent crime. You have survived, you're alive to read this, and you shall overcome your current feelings of trauma and hurt.

I don't mean to sound like Ralph Edwards, the host of the T.V. show entitled <u>This is Your Life</u>, but this is your life! Allow people into your life to assist in your recovery process. Allow yourself to feel whatever you need to feel. You have survived an ordeal that certainly threatened your happiness and perhaps your life. Go forward in growing toward completion of your recovery process and live your life fully, because remember…YOU ARE A SURVIVOR!

APPENDIX

STATE COALITION PHONE NUMBERS
These numbers are correct be you a male or female.

- Alabama Coalition Against Domestic Violence— (334)832-4842
- Alaska Network on Domestic Violence & Sexual Assault—(907)586-3650
- Arizona Coalition Against Domestic Violence— (602)279-2900
- Arkansas Coalition Against Domestic Violence—(800) 269-4668
- California Alliance Against Domestic Violence— (916) 444-7163
- Statewide California Coalition for Battered Women— (888) 722-2952
- Colorado Coalition Against Domestic Violence— (303) 831-9632
- Connecticut Coalition Against Domestic Violence— (860) 282-7899
- Delaware Coalition Against Domestic Violence— (302) 658-2958
- DC Coalition Against Domestic Violence— (202) 299-1181
- Florida Coalition Against Domestic Violence— (850) 425-2749
- Georgia Coalition against Domestic Violence— (404)209- 0280
- Georgia Crisis Line (800)334-2836

- Hawaii State Coalition Against Domestic Violence—(808)832-9316
- Idaho Coalition Against Sexual and Domestic Violence—(208) 384-0419
- Illinois Coalition Against Domestic Violence—(217) 789-2830
- Indiana Coalition Against Domestic Violence—(317)917-3685
- Iowa Coalition Against Domestic Violence—(515) 244-8028
- Kansas Coalition Against Sexual & Domestic Violence—(785) 232-9784
- Kentucky Domestic Violence Association—(502) 695-2444
- Louisiana Coalition Against Domestic Violence—(888)411-1333
- Maine Coalition for Family Crisis Services—(207) 941-1194
- Maryland Network Against Domestic Violence—(301) 352-4574
- Massachusetts Coalition of Battered Women's Service Groups—(617) 248-0922
- Michigan Coalition Against Domestic Violence—(517) 347-7000
- Minnesota Coalition for Battered Women—(651)646-0994
- Mississippi Coalition Against Domestic Violence—(601) 981-9196
- Missouri Coalition Against Domestic Violence—(573) 634-4161
- Montana Coalition Against Domestic Violence—(406) 443-7794

- Nebraska Domestic Violence and Sexual Assault Coalition—(402) 476-6256
- Nevada Network Against Domestic Violence—(800)500-1556
- New Hampshire Coalition Against Domestic and Sexual Violence—(603) 224-8893
- New Jersey Coalition for Battered Women—(609) 584-8107
- New Mexico State Coalition Against Domestic Violence—(505) 246-9240
- New York State Coalition Against Domestic Violence—(800)942-6906
- North Carolina Coalition Against Domestic Violence—(919) 956-9124
- North Dakota Council on Abused Women's Services –(701) 255-6240
- Ohio Domestic Violence Network—(800)934-9840
- Action Ohio Coalition for Battered Women—(614)221-1255
- Oklahoma Coalition on Domestic Violence and Sexual Assault—(405) 848-1815
- Oregon Coalition Against Domestic and Sexual Violence—(503) 365-9644
- Pennsylvania Coalition Against Domestic Violence—(717) 545-6400
- Comision Para Los Asuntos De La Mujer, Puerto Rico—(787) 722-2907
- Rhode Island Council on Domestic Violence—(401) 467-9940
- South Carolina Coalition Against Domestic Violence & Sexual Assault—(803) 256-2900
- South Dakota Coalition Against Domestic Violence & Sexual Assault—(605) 945-0869

- Tennessee Task Force Against Family Violence—
  (615) 386-9406
- Texas Council on Family Violence—(512) 794-1133
- Utah Domestic Violence Information Line—
  (800)897-5465
- Vermont Network Against Domestic Violence and
  Sexual Assault—(802) 223-1302
- Virginians Against Domestic Violence—
  (757) 221-0990
- Washington State Domestic Violence Hotline—
  (800)562-6025
- West Virginia Coalition Against Domestic Violence—
  (304) 965-3552
- Wisconsin Coalition Against Domestic Violence—
  (608) 255-0539
- Wyoming Coalition Against Domestic Violence and
  Sexual Assault—(307) 755-5481
- Women's Resource Center, Virgin Islands—
  (809) 776-3966
- Women's Coalition of St. Croix, Virgin Islands—
  (340) 773-9272